TO OUR

GREAT

FRIENDSHIP

GN00706102

V&R
PUBLISHERS

IN PRAISE
OF
FRIENDSHIP

How was friendship born?
Surely as an alliance before
adversity, an alliance
without which man would
have been left
disarmed in life.

MILAN KUNDERA

It is so small a thing
To have enjoyed the sun,
To have lived light in the spring,
To have loved, to have thought,
To have done, to have
Advanced true friends.

MATTHEW ARNOLD

Love is a sudden blaze, which soon decays;
Friendship is like the sun's eternal rays;
Not daily benefits exhaust the flame;
It still is giving, and still burns the same.

JOHN GAY

Friendship knows the exact
time for words and
the exact time for silence.

FERNÁNDEZ LAFUENTE

If we dream it alone,
a dream is just a dream.
But if we dream it with our
friends, it will be the beginning
of something real.

HELDER CAMARA

Those who bring sunshine
to the lives of others
cannot keep it
from themselves.

J. M. BARRIE

We are all travellers in the
wilderness of this world,
and the best that we find in our
travels is an honest friend.

ROBERT LOUIS STEVENSON

True happiness consists not
in a multitude of friends,
but in the worth and choice...
Let them be good that love me,
though but few.

SAMUEL JOHNSON

What sunshine is to flowers, smiles are to humanity.
They are but trifles, to be sure, but scattered along
life's pathway, the good they do is inconceivable.

JOSEPH ADDISON

But if the while I think on thee, dear friend,
All losses are restored, and sorrows end.

WILLIAM SHAKESPEARE

There is in friendship something of all relations, and
something above them all. It is the golden thread
that ties the hearts of all the world.

JOHN EVELYN

My friends have made the story of my life. In a thousand ways they have turned my limitations into beautiful privileges, and enabled me to walk serene and happy in the shadow cast by my deprivation.

HELEN KELLER

Some of the most rewarding and beautiful moments of a friendship happen in the unforeseen open spaces between planned activities. It is important that you allow these spaces to exist.

CHRISTINE LEEFELDT

Not to be wanted or loved,
to be forgotten by all is a greater
hunger and a greater poverty
than having nothing to eat.
But a touch of love is enough
to cure loneliness, because creating
a relationship, having a friend
consoles that hunger.

MOTHER TERESA OF CALCUTTA

There is a space within
sisterhood for likeness and
difference, for the subtle
differences that challenge and
delight; there is space for
disappointment – and surprise.

CHRISTINE DOWNING

15

One should choose friends as one chooses books. Succeeding does not mean you've found many, nor that they're extraordinary, but rather that they are few, good and so very familiar.

MATEO ALEMÁN

Friendship is the relinquishment of selfishness and the sum of generosities.

JOAQUÍN A. PEÑALOZA

It is a hug of forgiveness, applause that urges you on, an encounter that delights you, a favor without compensation. It is giving with no demands, committing with no calculation. It is waiting… tirelessly.

CECILIA PREZIOSO

The glory of friendship
is not the outstretched hand,
nor the kindly smile,
nor the joy of companionship;
it is the spiritual inspiration
that comes to one when he
discovers that someone believes
and is willing to trust him
with his friendship.

RALPH W. EMERSON

Friendship is unnecessary,
like philosophy, like art...
It has no survival value;
rather it is one of those things
that give value to survival.

C. S. LEWIS

There is no friend like an old friend
Who has shared our morning days,
No greeting like his welcome,
No homage like his praise.

OLIVER WENDELL HOLMES

The world is empty if one thinks only of mountains,
rivers, and cities; but to know someone here and
there who thinks and feels with us, and who,
though distant, is close to us in spirit,
this makes the earth an inhabited garden.

JOHANN W. GOETHE

One man in a thousand, Solomon says,
Will stick more close than a brother.
And it's worthwhile seeking him half your days
If you find him before the other.

Nine hundred and ninety-nine depend
On what the world sees in you,
But the Thousandth man will stand your friend
With the whole round world against you.

His wrong's your wrong, and his right's your right,
In season or out of season.
Stand up and back it in all men's sight –
With that for your only reason!

Nine hundred and ninety-nine can't bide
The shame or mocking or laughter,
But the Thousandth Man will stand by your side
To the gallows-foot – and after!

RUDYARD KIPLING

THE
VALUE
OF
FRIENDSHIP

Friendship as the union
of two selves lies beyond
happiness or unhappiness.
It is simply the other side
of our life and thus,
free from all danger.

LADISLAUS BOROS

One's life has value so long
as one attributes value to the life of others
by means of love, friendship,
and compassion.

SIMONE DE BEAUVOIR

The bird, a nest;
The spider, a web;
Man, friendship.

WILLIAM BLAKE

There is nothing we like to see so much
as the gleam of pleasure in a person's eye
when he feels that we have sympathized
with him, understood him,
interested ourselves in his welfare.
At these moments something fine and spiritual
passes between two friends.
These moments are the moments worth living.

DON MARQUIS

Let friendship fly free
like a butterfly, and alight
from one heart to another.
If you shut it away, it can
no longer spread its wings.
If you confine a friendship,
it will suffocate.

WILLIAM PENN

Here is the one true reason
for friendship: to offer a mirror in
which the other can contemplate
his reflection of yesteryear
which, without the memory
of companions, would have
faded away over time.

MILAN KUNDERA

May the road
rise to meet you.

May the wind
be always at your back.

May the sun shine
warm upon your face
and the rain fall soft
upon your fields.

And until we meet again,
may God hold you
in the hollow of His hand.

IRISH BLESSING

Friendship consists in forgetting what one gives,
and remembering what one receives.

ALEXANDRE DUMAS

The only service a friend can really render is
to keep up your courage by holding up to you
a mirror in which you can see a noble image
of yourself.

GEORGE BERNARD SHAW

My friends are my estate. Forgive me
then the avarice to hoard them!

EMILY DICKINSON

THE JOY OF FRIENDSHIP

Tear down the wall that
isolates you and with the
bricks build a bridge
to reach your friend.

JOAQUÍN A. PEÑALOZA

I breathed a song into the air,
It fell to earth, I knew not where;
For, who has sight so keen and strong
That it can follow the flight of song?

Long, long afterward, in an oak
I found the arrow, still unbroke;
And the song, from beginning to end,
I found again in the heart of a friend.

HENRY WADSWORTH LONGFELLOW

Pain can take care of itself, but to squeeze
everything out of joy, you've got to have someone
with whom to share it.

MARK TWAIN

And a youth said to the Prophet,
Speak to us of Friendship.

And he answered, saying:

Let there be no purpose
in friendship save the
deepening of the spirit.

For love that seeks aught but
the disclosure of its own mystery
is not love but a net cast forth:
and only the unprofitable is caught.

And let your best be for your friend.

If he must know the ebb of your
tide, let him know
its flood also.

For what is your friend that you
should seek him
with hours to kill?

Seek him always with hours to live.

For it is his to fill your need,
but not your emptiness.

And in the sweetness of friendship
let there be laughter,
and sharing of pleasures.

For in the dew of little things
the heart finds its morning
and is refreshed.

KAHLIL GIBRAN

Each one of us is an angel
with just one wing,
and will only be able to fly
if we embrace one another.

LUCIANO OF CRESCENSO

On the level of the human spirit
an equal, a companion,
and an understanding heart
is one who can share
a man's point of view.
Those, who feel for us
as we feel for ourselves,
who are bound to us
in triumph and disaster,
who break the spell
of our loneliness.

HENRY ALONZO MYERS

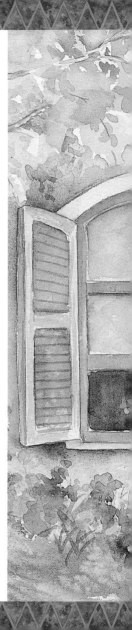

Each friend represents a world
in us, a world possibly not born
until they arrive, and it is only
by this meeting
that a new world is born.

ANAÏS NIN

The making of friends, who are
real friends, is the best token we
have of a man's success in life.

EDWARD EVERETT HALE

True friendship comes when
silence between two people
is easy and comfortable.

DAVE TYSON GENTRY

It is the human touch in the world that counts –
The touch of your hand and mine.
Which means far more to the sinking heart
Than shelter or bread or wine.
For shelter is gone when the night is over,
And bread lasts only a day.
But the touch of the hand and the sound of the voice
Live on in the soul always.

SPENCER M. FREE

We cannot tell the precise moment when friendship is formed. As in filling a vessel drop by drop, there is at last a drop which makes the heart run over.

JAMES BOSWELL

Advice is like snow; the softer it falls, the longer it dwells upon, and the deeper it sinks into the mind.

SAMUEL TAYLOR COLERIDGE

I want to be your friend forever,
without pause or discouragement.
Until the hills become level
and the rivers dry up; until it
thunders and snows in Summer.
When the sky and the earth
come together,
only then will I abandon you.

CHINESE TEXT

Today a man discovered gold
    and fame,
Another flew the stormy seas;
One found the germ of a
    disease.
But what high fates my path
    attend:
For I – today – I found a friend.

HELEN BAKER PARKER

May the trail of the wind
leave its songs in your path,
May the sun light the sky where
        you stand;
May the pleasure of friendship be
        yours through the days,
With a clasp of a caring hand.

VIRGINIA COVEY BOSWELL

The communicating of a man's
self to his friend worketh two
contrary effects, for it
redoubleth joys, and cutteth
griefs in halfs; for there is no man
that imparteth his joys to his
friend, but he rejoyeth the more,
and no man that imparteth his
grief to his friend,
but he grieveth the less.

FRANCIS BACON

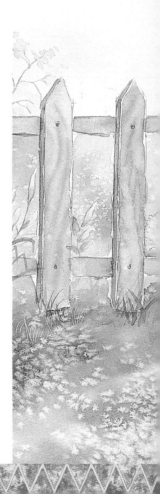

From quiet homes and first beginning,
Out to the undiscovered end,
There is nothing worth the wear of winning,
But laughter and the love of friends.

HILAIRE BELLOC

Beautiful and rich is an old friendship,
grateful to the touch as ancient ivory,
smoothed as aged wine,
or sheen tapestry where light has lingered,
intimate and long.

EUNICE TIETJENS

No love, no friendship can cross
the path of our destiny without leaving
some mark on it forever.

FRANÇOIS MAURIAC